ROCK PICTURE CHORDS AND HOW TO USE THEM.

By Mark Michaels.

Book design by Mark Stein

© Amsco Music Publishing Company
A Division of Music Sales Corporation, 1978
33 West 60th Street, New York 10023
All Rights Reserved

Music Sales Limited
78 Newman Street, London W1

Music Sales (Pty) Limited
27 Clarendon Street, Artarmon, Sydney NSW, Australia

International Standard Book Number: 0 86001 892 X
Order NO. AM 21718

Printed & Bound by J.B. Offset Printers (Marks Tey) Ltd.
Station Approach, North Lane, Marks Tey,
Colchester, Essex.

Introduction

This book is designed to teach you, in a clear and easy way, the chords and progressions you will need to play songs in the rock idiom. Through the use of pictures and diagrams, the basic chords in each key become easily recognized and immediately useful.

Rock Picture Chords can be used as a step-by-step learning method, as a chord reference book or as a practice guide to help strengthen your chord technique. Some popular tunes have been added for both their interest and for the practical application of the chords shown. *Rock Picture Chords* starts with the simplest and most common first position chords and progresses quickly to more complex chords, including bar chords and other movable patterns.

For best results, the beginner should proceed systematically, making sure he or she plays all the practice progressions and memorizes every chord, playing them until they can be fretted accurately and quickly. Once the chords in a particular key are learned thoroughly, they should be applied to the songs presented in this book as well as other rock songs. The student is encouraged to learn as many songs from records, the radio and other books as he or she can. Also, there is no substitute for private instruction and communication between fellow musicians.

This book will not only be useful in playing rock guitar but it will increase your knowledge and technique for playing other kinds of music on the instrument, such as blues, jazz and folk.

How to Use
This Book

The information presented in this book is given in the same form for every two pages. Each time you open the book, you will find that the left and right-hand pages make up a unit. Each unit is comprised of three or more chord diagrams, a number of Checkpoints, a Rhythm Pattern written in tablature, three Practice Progressions and a popular song.

The chord diagram is a picture of the guitar finger-board in map form. The six vertical lines represent the six strings (E, A, D, G, B, E from highest to lowest) and the horizontal lines represent the frets. Circles indicate the place at which the string is fretted and the number indicates the finger of the left hand used to fret. The following key is standard: 1 = middle finger, 3 = ring finger and 4 = little finger. Each diagram is drawn as if the guitar were facing you in a vertical position. Therefore, the sixth or low E string is on the left and the first or high E string is on the right.

The Checkpoints following the chord diagrams should be read and adhered to. The Rhythm Pattern is an example of what you might play in a particular rock tune. You can use it to play the Practice Progressions or you can use a previously given Rhythm Pattern. For this reason, the Rhythm Pattern given within all of the Practice Progressions is one strum (stroke) per beat—that is, four strums per measure, although you will be playing something which is actually quite a bit more complex.

The song given at the end of each unit is for fun and practice. Usually, the whole song is not given, just the first verse or chorus. Also, the songs are generally not in the keys they were in originally.

How to Hold the Guitar

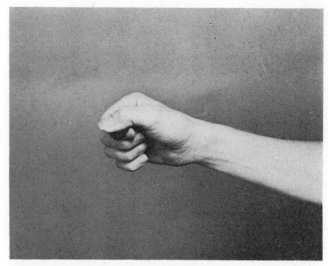

How to Hold the Pick (Plectrum)

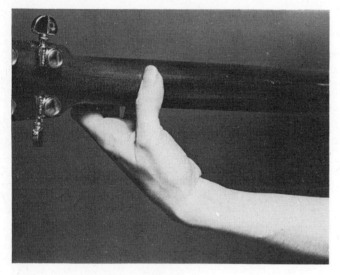

How to Hold Your Left Hand

How to Strum with Your Right Hand

Key of E

E

A

B⁷

Checkpoints

—Be sure to play only the notes for which left-hand notation is given. Do not play the strings which have an "X" above them.

—Play the open strings so that they ring clearly. Remember to arch your left hand around the neck of the guitar.

—Play the rhythms slowly so that the sound is steady and even. Increase your speed until the song is in the right tempo.

Rhythm Pattern

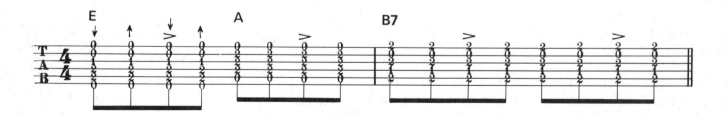

Practice Progressions

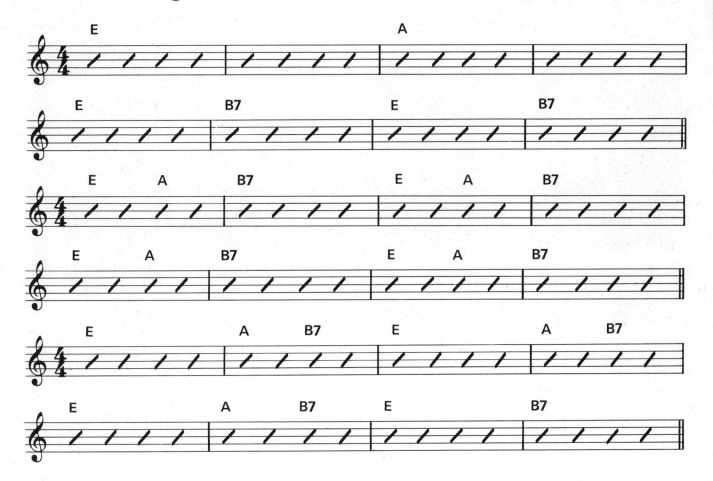

Rain

Lennon/McCartney

If the rain comes they run and hide their heads they might as well be dead if the rain comes, _____ if the rain comes.

Key of A

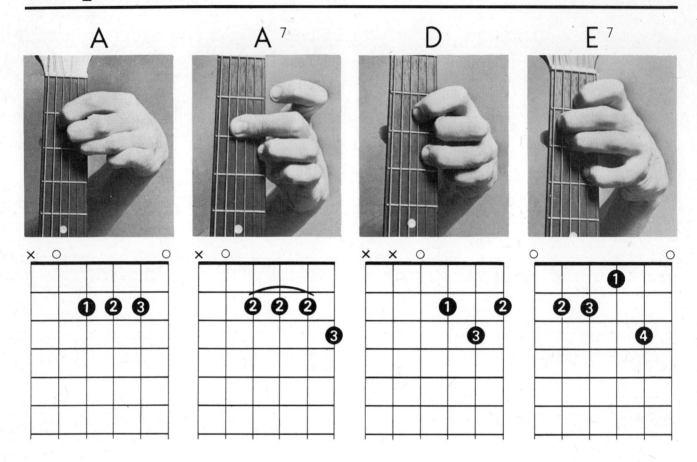

Checkpoints

—Play whichever chord fingering is most comfortable for you and allows you to change to the next chord the fastest.

—Be sure that each note in the chord rings clear. Press down firmly just before the fret bar in order to get the clearest tone.

Rhythm Pattern

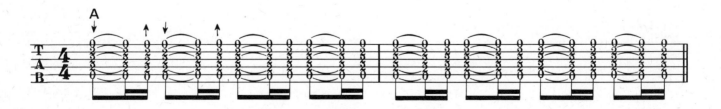

Practice Progressions

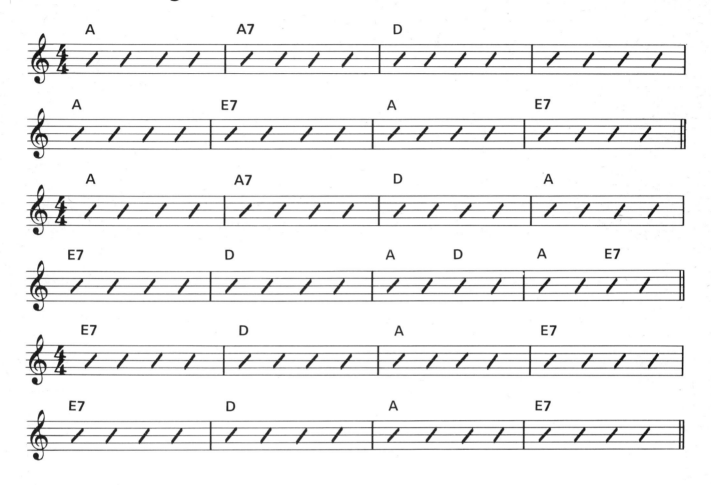

Stagger Lee

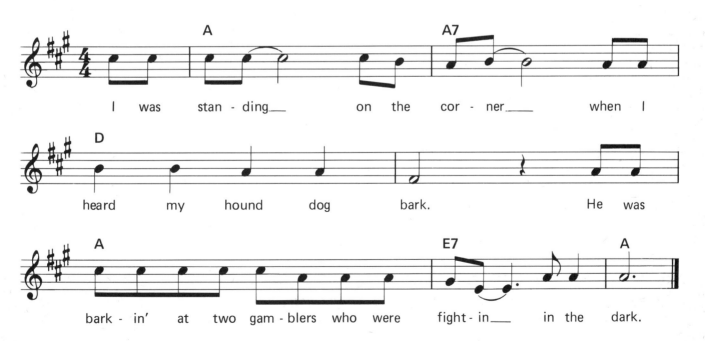

I was stan - ding___ on the cor - ner___ when I heard my hound dog bark. He was bark - in' at two gam - blers who were fight - in___ in the dark.

Key of D

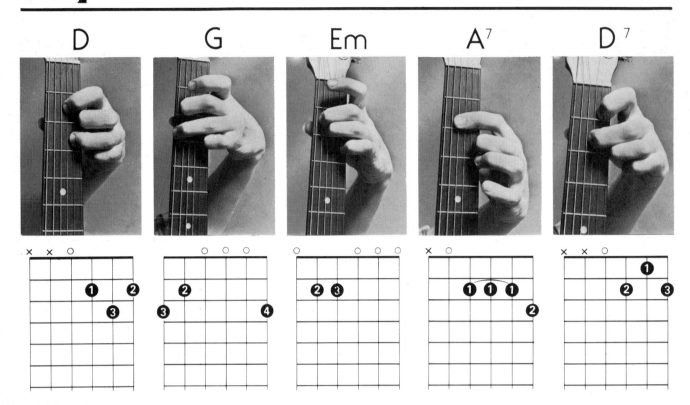

D   G   Em   A⁷   D⁷

Checkpoints

—You can play the other forms of A^7 given previously as well as this one.

—Strum across the soundhole if you are using an acoustic guitar or between the bridge and the end of the fingerboard (between the pickups) if you are practicing on an electric guitar.

Rhythm Pattern

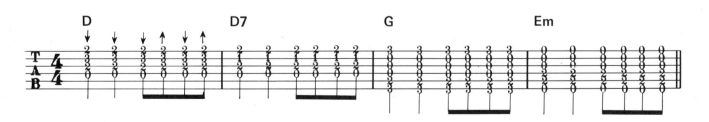

Practice Progressions

Key of D

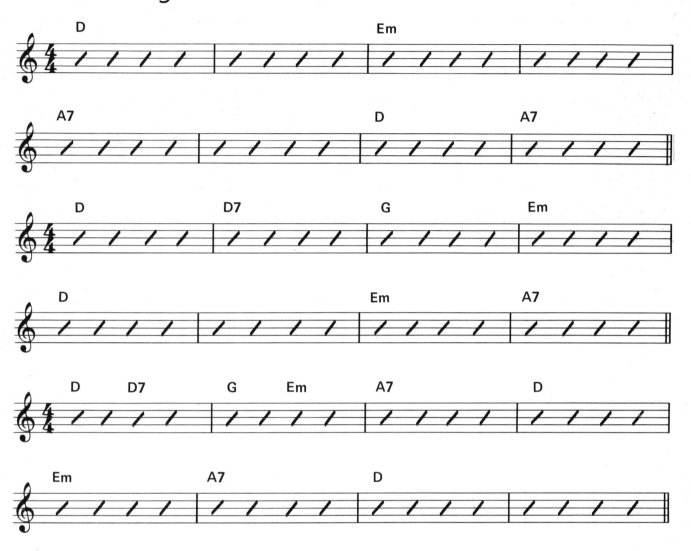

Don't Let Me Down

Lennon/McCartney

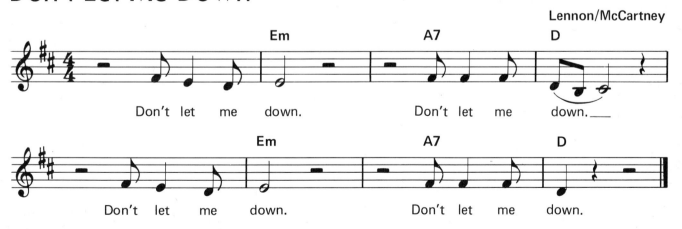

Don't let me down. Don't let me down.

Don't let me down. Don't let me down.

Key of G

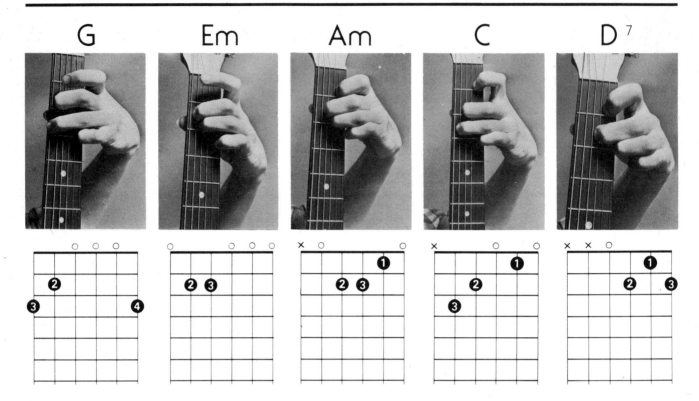

G   Em   Am   C   D⁷

Checkpoints

—After playing for a while, check your guitar to be sure that it is still in tune with itself. It is quite normal for a guitar to go out of tune slightly after it has been played for a while.

—Press down *hard* with your left hand. You don't have to press until it hurts but the reward is that callouses will develop on the fingertips of your left hand and this will eventually make it easier to finger difficult chords.

Rhythm Pattern

This kind of rhythm is known as a "stop rhythm".
Use it to play the accompanying song.

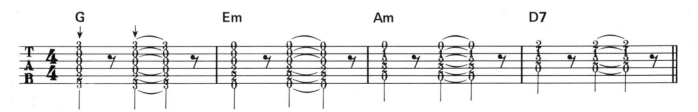

Practice Progressions

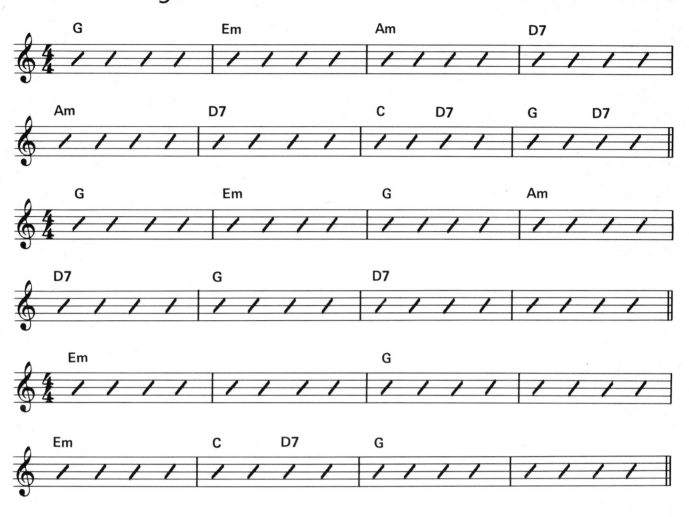

Anna

Arthur Alexander

An - na,___ you come an' ask me, girl___

to set you free, girl._____ You say he loves you

more than me, so I will set you free; go with him.

Key of C

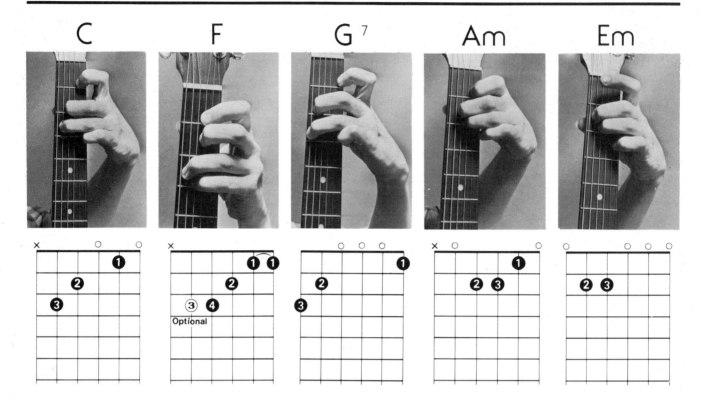

Checkpoints

—Press hard with the first (index) finger when playing the F chord. Be sure that all of the notes sound clearly.

—Don't let your left hand accidentally touch the open strings when playing the C or G^7. Remember to arch your left hand around the neck.

Rhythm Pattern

This pattern gives you plenty of time to change from one chord to the next because the last beat of the measure is not played.

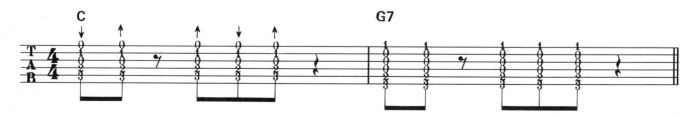

Practice Progressions

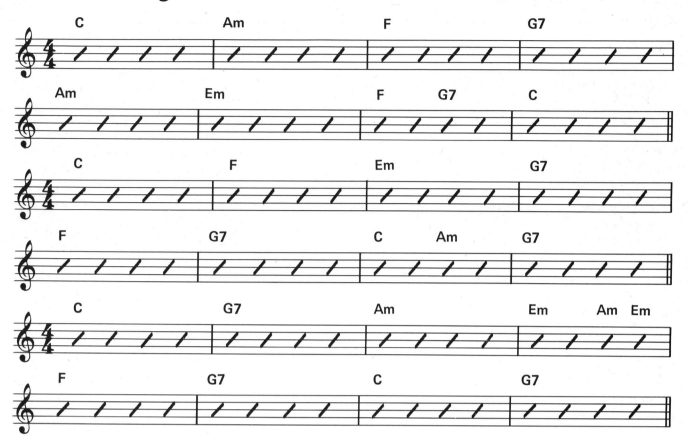

Frankie and Johnny

Frank-ie and John-ny were lov-ers,___ Lord-y, how they___ could

love. Swore to be true___ to each oth-er,___ just as

true as the stars a-bove, He was her man,_____

___ but he___ done her wrong._____

Key of F

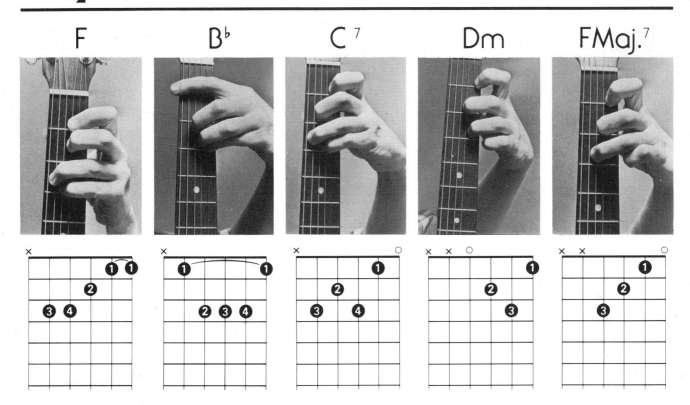

F   B♭   C⁷   Dm   FMaj.⁷

Checkpoints

—When playing the F chord, press the thumb tightly against the back of the neck to exert pressure on the strings. This will eventually develop your hand and wrist.

—Also, keep your index finger flat so as to fret both the 1st and 2nd strings. This applies to both the F and B♭ chords.

—Touch the high E (first) string lightly with the loose skin of your left palm if you want to mute the string instead of having it sound.

—The FMaj.7 chord can often be used as a substitute chord for the F Major. Major seventh chords give you a jazzier or more mellow sound than the regular major chords. With the FMaj.7, the high E string must be played open.

Rhythm Pattern

Practice Progressions

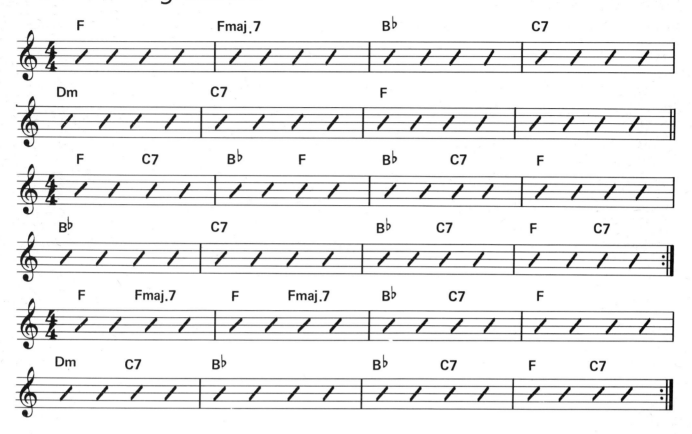

What You're Doing

Lennon/McCartney

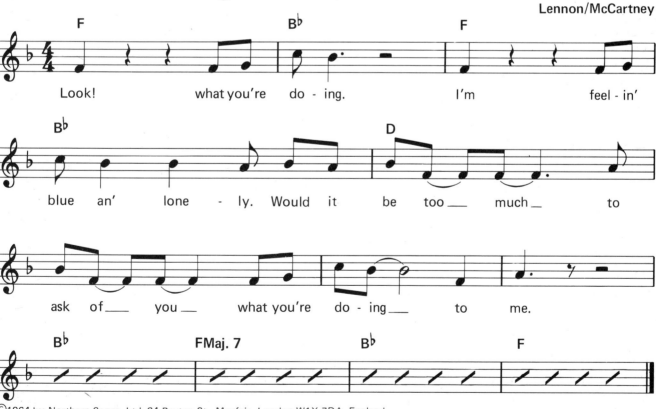

Look! what you're do-ing. I'm feel-in'

blue an' lone-ly. Would it be too ___ much ___ to

ask of ___ you ___ what you're do-ing ___ to me.

Key of Am

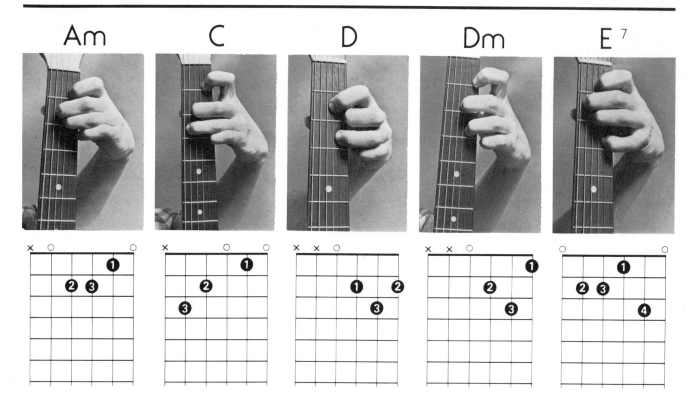

Am   C   D   Dm   E⁷

Checkpoints

—This key is the relative minor to the key of C major. Every major key has a relative minor key. Both keys have certain chords in common. Minor keys generally have a more sombre or blue sound to them than do major keys.

—Keep the fingernails of your left hand trim and clean.

Rhythm Pattern

The second rhythm pattern is written in 3/4 time instead of 4/4. That means that you count three beats to the measure instead of four.

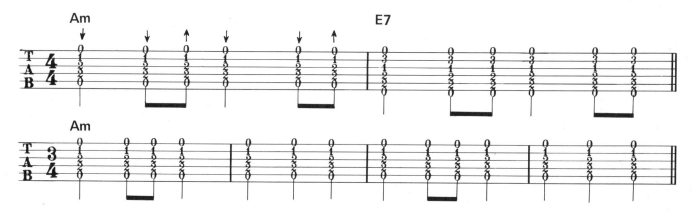

Practice Progressions

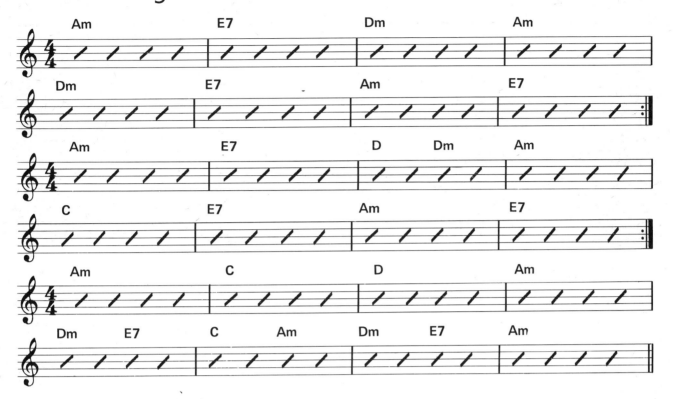

House of the Rising Sun

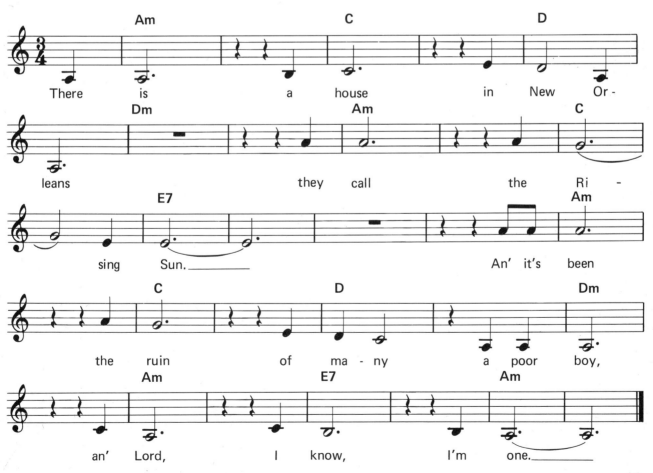

There is a house in New Or-
leans they call the Ri-
sing Sun. An' it's been
the ruin of ma-ny a poor boy,
an' Lord, I know, I'm one.

Bar Chords

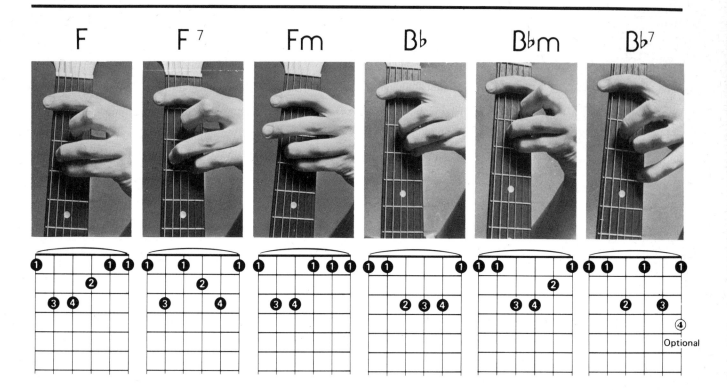

F F⁷ Fm B♭ B♭m B♭⁷

Optional

Checkpoints

—Press down firmly with your index finger so as to make the notes played sound clear.

—These chords may be moved to any position on the fingerboard. Each fret up the neck raises the chord by half a tone. Therefore, the E position with the bar on the 2nd fret is an F♯; on the 3rd fret it's a G and so on.

Rhythm Pattern

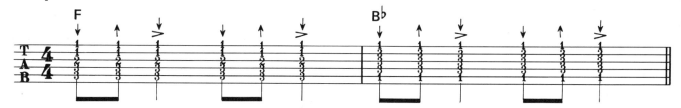

Practice Progressions

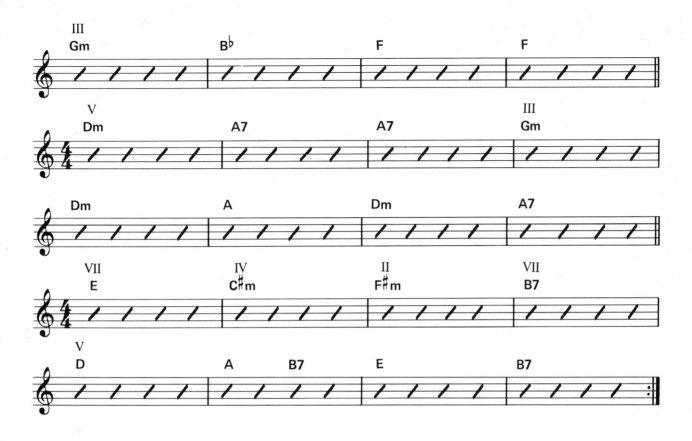

Sergeant Pepper's Lonely Hearts Club Band

Lennon/McCartney

Bar Chords

It was twen-ty years a-go to-day that Ser-geant

Pep-per taught the band to play. They've been go-ing in and out of

style, but they're guar-an-teed to raise a smile. So

may I in-tro-duce to you the act you've known for all these

years, Ser-geant Pep-per's Lone-ly-hearts Club Band.___

Minor Seventh Chords

Cm⁷ Gm⁷ Bm⁷

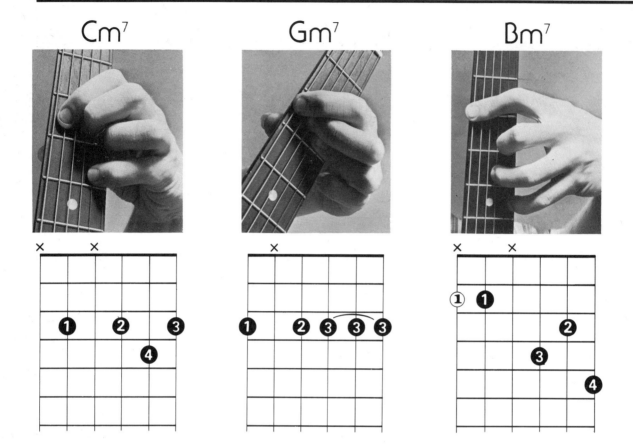

Checkpoints

—These chords are movable. For every fret you go up the neck, the chord is raised by ½ step.

—Minor seventh chords are very useful in all kinds of music. Often they can be used instead of (substituted for) the regular minor chords.

—Remember to strum across the soundhole to get the best sound.

—On the Cm7, mute the fourth string with your index finger, on the Gm7, mute the fifth string with your index finger and on the Bm7, mute the fourth string with your index finger.

Rhythm Pattern

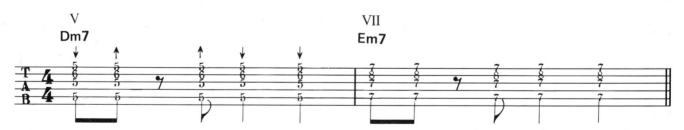

Practice Progressions

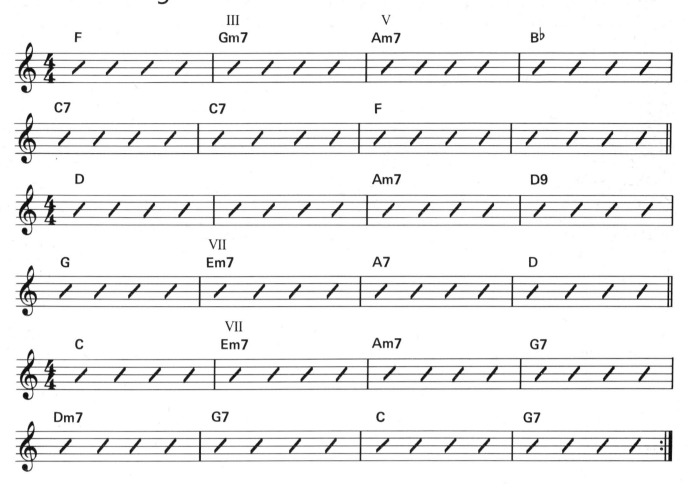

Here, There and Everywhere

Lennon/McCartney

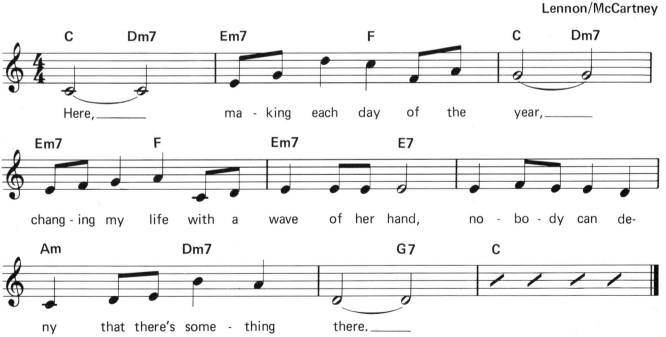

Minor
Sevenths

More Movable Chords

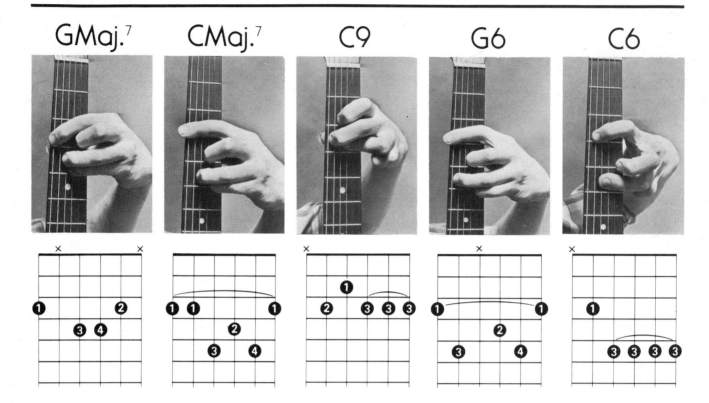

GMaj.7   CMaj.7   C9   G6   C6

Checkpoints

—Mute the 1st(E) and the 5th(A) strings on the GMaj.7 chord with the first finger so that they will not sound.

—Mute the 5th(A) string on the G6 chord with the 3rd finger.

—Keep your index finger as straight as possible when barring.

Rhythm Pattern

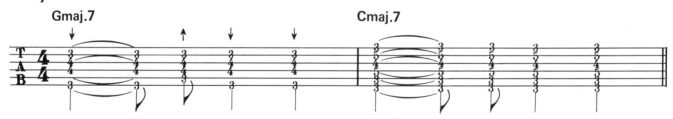

Practice Progressions

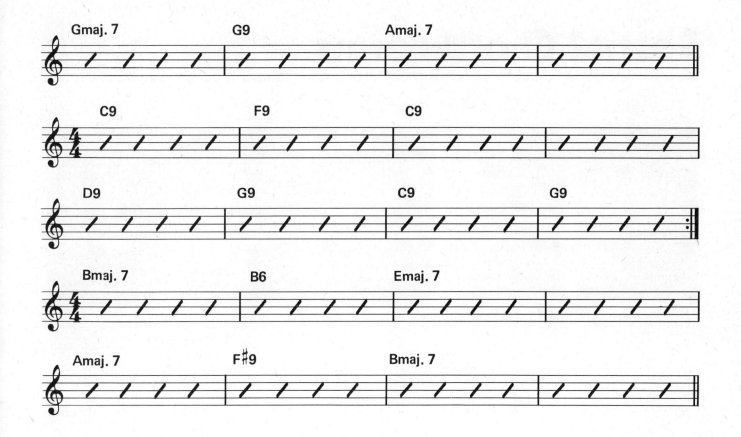

Easy Life

D.C. al Fine

More
Movable
Chords

Partial Chord Forms

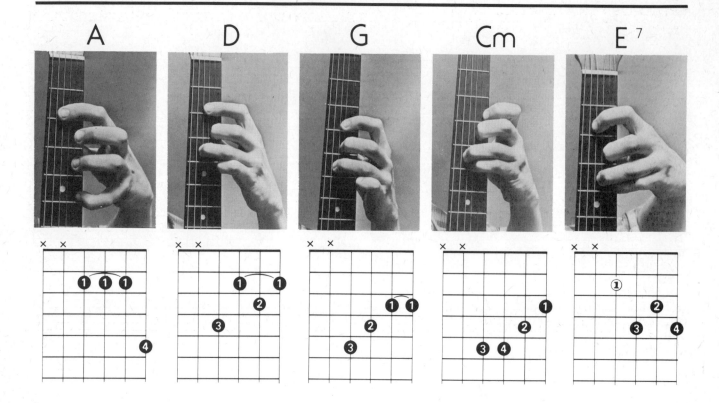

A   D   G   Cm   E⁷

Checkpoints

—All of these chords can be played in any position (fret) along the fingerboard.

—The accent here is on the high (treble) strings so be sure that you don't accidentally play one of the bass (low) strings if you are not supposed to.

Rhythm Pattern

Practice Progressions

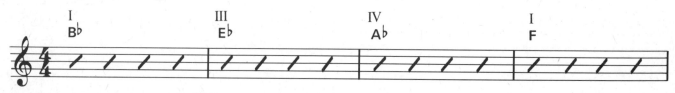

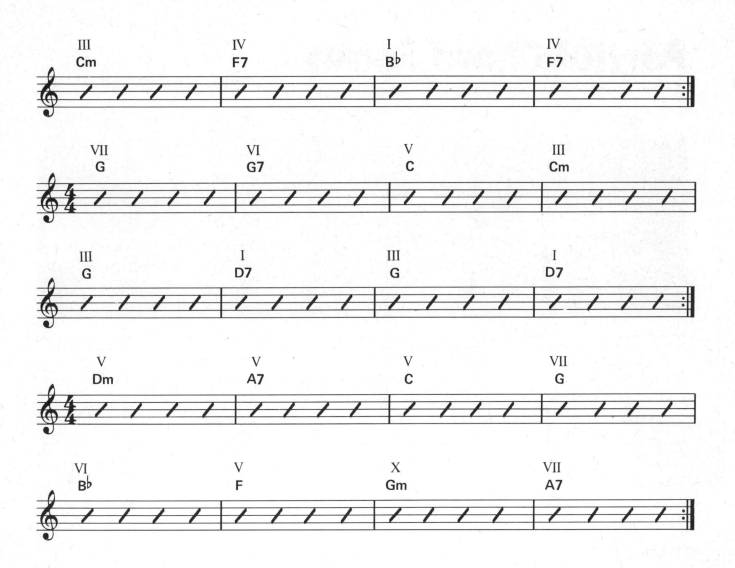

And Your Bird Can Sing

Lennon/McCartney

Tell me that you've got e-very-thing you want,— and your bird can sing, but you don't get me, you don't get me.

Partial Chord Forms

Augmented Chords

F+(A+,C#+)   F#+(Bb+,D+)   G+(B+,Eb+)   G#+(C+,E+)

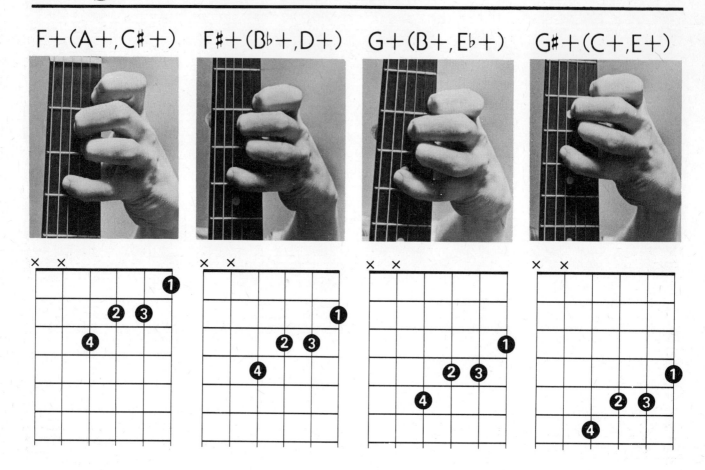

Checkpoints

—These chords are movable. For every fret you go up, you get three new augmented chords.

—These chords are generally used as passing chords to move up a fourth from whatever chord you are playing. For example, G → G+ → C or D → D+ → G.

—The two bass strings are not played on these augmented chords.

Rhythm Pattern

Practice Progressions

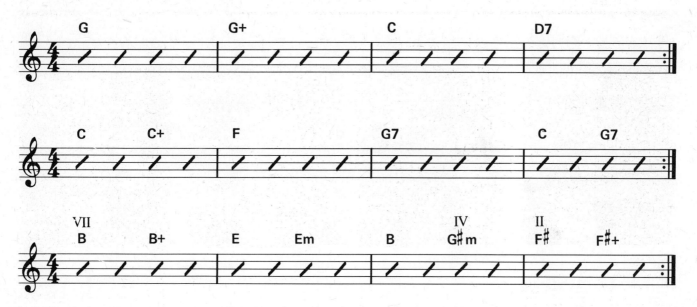

I'll Follow the Sun

Lennon/McCartney

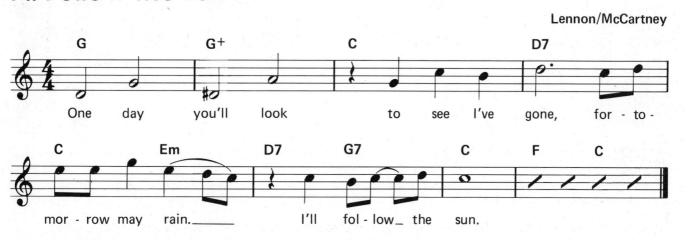

One day you'll look to see I've gone, for to-mor-row may rain.____ I'll fol-low_ the sun.

Aug-mented

Diminished Chords

A −, C −, D#−/E♭−, F#−/G♭−

A#−/B♭−, C#−/D♭−, E −, G −

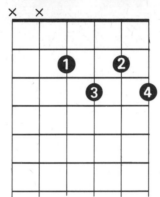

B −, D −, F −, G#−/A♭−

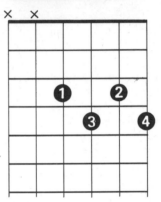

Checkpoints

—These chords are movable. You can move them up the neck as long as you do not play the two bass strings. For every fret you go up, you get three new diminished chords.

—Remember to keep the fingers of your left hand arched so that all of the notes will sound clear.

—Diminished chords are not used extensively in rock songs but they are good to know how to play for when they do appear.

Rhythm Pattern

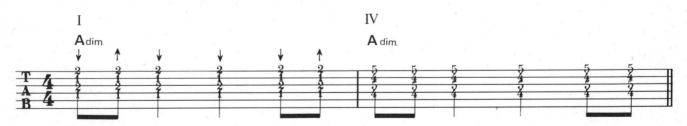

Practice Progressions

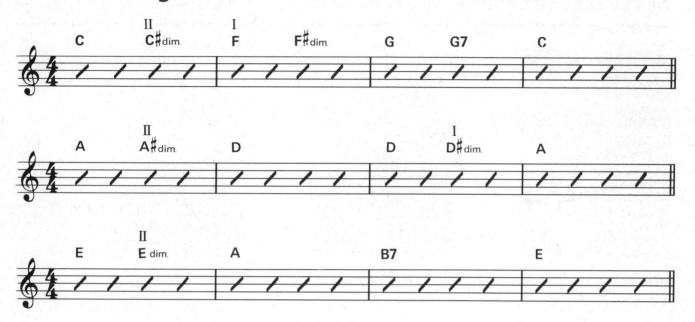

Michelle

Lennon/McCartney

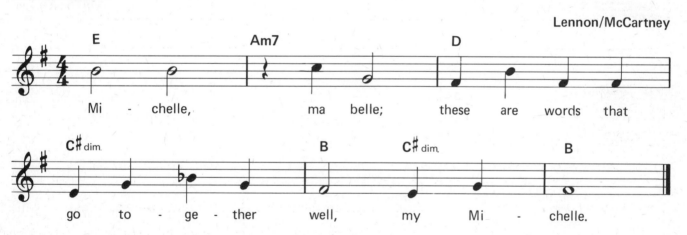

Mi - chelle, ma belle; these are words that go to - ge - ther well, my Mi - chelle.

Dimin-
ished

Let these OAK books help you pick something new